Dorothy M. Stewart brings a remarkably appropriate ragbag of experience to this book. She is herself a full-time family carer for her husband, who suffers from dementia as a result of multiple sclerosis. She is a lay preacher in the United Reformed Church and has a solid foundation in communicating the word of God to encourage, support and strengthen others.

She has had a career in book publishing, at Ahmadu Bello University Press (northern Nigeria), Macmillan Press, McGraw-Hill, Chartac Books (the publishing arm of the Institute of Chartered Accountants in England and Wales) and SPCK.

She has also had a number of books published: *Bluff Your Way in Publishing* (Ravette), *Women of Prayer* (Lion and Loyola), *Women of Spirit* (Lion and Loyola), *The Gower Handbook of Management Skills* (Gower/Ashgate), *The Westminster Collection of Christian Prayers* (Westminster John Knox Press), *It's Hard to Hurry When You're a Snail* (Lion) and *A Book of Graces* (SPCK). She is actively involved in relevant carers' support organizations.

D0281734

ONE DAY AT A TIME

Meditations for carers

Dorothy M. Stewart

First published in Great Britain in 2010

Society for Promoting Christian Knowledge
36 Causton Street
London SW1P 4ST

British Library Cataloguing-in-Publication Data
A catalogue record for this book is available from the British Library

ISBN 978-0-281-06172-3

1 3 5 7 9 10 8 6 4 2

Typeset by Graphicraft Ltd, Hong Kong
Printed in Great Britain by Ashford Colour Press

Produced on paper from sustainable forests

Contents

Contents

Acknowledgements

———◆◆◆———

Learning how to be a carer has been a rocky road for me but there have been helpful people and supportive organizations along the way. So it's good to have this opportunity to say thank you to: Dr Ashford, who diagnosed my husband's frontal lobe dementia and has maintained contact and reassessed John as necessary; Lucie Kerridge, our social worker, who has been a wonderful support; Suffolk Family Carers, especially Tracey Sharp, and Hayley and the Flexible Respite Team; David Gaffney at Margary & Miller, Southwold, our solicitor who dealt with the Enduring Power of Attorney; Paula and the team involved in the Halesworth CAD (Carers' Action for Dementia) group; Pat Cruse of the Alzheimer's Society; Aileen and the staff at Oaklands House in Reydon; Gerald and team at Carlton Hall; my stepchildren, Neil and Claudia Courtis, and my church, Halesworth United Reformed Church; and very specially, Gloria and Ian Richardson next door, and Margaret, George and Charlotte Long. And of course my husband John with whom I have walked this rocky road.

Introduction

The Alzheimer's Society estimates that there are currently 700,000 people with dementia in the UK. One-third of those live in care homes, which means that two-thirds (over 450,000) live 'in the community' – that is, in their own homes, with someone, usually a spouse, sibling or grown-up child, looking after them. And there are many other reasons for needing at-home care, either part-time or full-time. A whole raft of illnesses and disabilities, affecting people of every age, have a devastating effect on the family as a whole and the person who accepts the main task of caring in particular. It is currently estimated that there are six million family carers in the UK and that this number will rise to over three in five of the population (source: The Princess Royal Trust for Carers, 2008).

Because the work of the family carer happens mainly behind the doors of the home, it tends to be pretty invisible to the rest of society. Carers aren't a vocal lot – generally they're too tired! As the Government wakes up to how much family carers are saving the State, more provision is gradually being made, though it's still hard to find out about and access. The caring role is a minefield and most carers admit to frustration, stress, anger, lack of help from family and friends, depression, feeling taken for granted, need for financial help, exhaustion, loneliness and many other heartaches (source: The Princess Royal Trust for Carers survey, 2006).

When my husband was diagnosed with frontal lobe impairment due to multiple sclerosis, vascular dementia and possible early Alzheimer's disease, I realized that I needed something more from my daily Bible reading and quiet time with God –

something specifically relevant to my new role as a carer – and I couldn't find it in any available books or booklets. In desperation, I grabbed my notebook and Bible and began to write, every day, what I wished had been there for me.

As I become more involved in groups supporting carers, I am realizing how many carers there are and how great their needs are, though seldom mentioned or acknowledged. So I share this little book in the hope that God will use it to support all carers. Your burden is indeed heavy and sometimes feels unbearable. May you find comfort and encouragement, and the strength to go on.

ONE DAY AT A TIME

1

And the lucky winner is . . .

And God is faithful; he will not let you be tempted beyond
what you can bear. But when you are tempted, he will also
provide a way out so that you can stand up under it.

(1 Corinthians 10.13)

I'll never win the Lottery – because I never buy a Lottery ticket.
On the other hand, I didn't apply for this job of being a carer.
Did you? I don't think anyone applies. It just happens. A baby
is born needing extra care, a child has a severe accident or illness, a parent or spouse becomes ill – and you become the carer.
If it happened very suddenly, it's unlikely that you had time
really to think about it. If it came on gradually, you may not
have noticed what was happening until it was too late.

But your life has changed radically. Now you're on call
twenty-four hours a day, seven days a week. And unlike lorry
drivers with tachographs, you have nobody keeping an eye on
you to make sure you're having enough rest and time off. In
fact, the State pays you more, the more hours you put in! It's
easy – and normal – to feel trapped. To feel you've had something foisted on you. And then of course you feel guilty that
you're feeling this way, because you love the person you look
after, don't you . . .

But the love you took it for granted you were going to
give was of a different kind: the love of a parent for a child, the
love of a wife for a husband or vice versa, the love of a child
for a parent . . . not this 24/7 total responsibility for absolutely

everything. This is where carers get cross with the Bible verse at the start of this chapter, because it simply doesn't seem to be true in their lives. I admit, I've felt that way too – but then a week later, a month later, I realize it was true. If we ask, God will give us the strength we need to do this task we never asked for. If we lean on him, he won't let us break under the strain.

Prayer

Dear Lord Jesus, you did not deserve to die on the cross but you endured that agony for us. Help us to endure the suffering that has come to us. Let us be aware of your encircling loving arms, your protection and your amazing provision for us. Take away any bitterness or resentment we feel about this caring role and fill our hearts with your love that it may spread into our day.

Self-care suggestion

If you're having a bad day and feeling bitter and resentful (and guilty!), go somewhere you can't be overheard and shout at God. Tell him exactly how you feel. There's some great stuff in Psalms 54 to 57 you could use. It helps to know that other people have been there before us! God won't be offended. He loves you.

2

Coming out

———•◆•———

The LORD is my light and my salvation; I will fear no one.
The LORD protects me from all danger; I will never be
afraid . . . even if enemies attack me, I will still trust God.
(Psalm 27.1, 3b, GNB)

Other people's reactions are unpredictable. Some folk are lovely
and supportive: they tell me they've encountered the problem
before, and add, 'So please don't worry.' The best of them reassure me of our welcome. They explain the special facilities
that are available to make life easier.

Some share their experiences as carers, or the stories of
people they've known in the caring role. One friend realized
just too late that her story was going to include the death of
her friend's mother and stopped sharply in case it upset me.
But that wouldn't have upset me. What upsets me is denial.

Once upon a time, nobody spoke about the illnesses and disabilities we're dealing with on a daily basis. It was all hidden
behind closed doors and families struggled on as best they
could. Thankfully, that has changed. But some people still shy
away from us and our loved ones. What we need are friends who
don't. And that's one of the benefits of our situation – it's easy
to see who our real friends are. They are pure gold!

Prayer
Thank you, Lord, for the people it's safe to be completely open
with. Teach me wisdom and discretion in who I tell what to.

There are people who feel threatened by our situation, who may respond in unhelpful ways. Help them too. And remind me that you love us whether we are carers or the person cared for. Your love remains constant, unshakeable and we can safely 'come out' to you.

Self-care suggestion

When someone treats you unkindly, ignores you or your loved one, says something hurtful or is just downright unhelpful, then when you get home and have a moment, write it down in a journal – for your eyes only. Or write a letter to God about what happened and how you feel. Get as angry as you need. Let it all come out. You'll feel much better!

3

Danger! Unexploded bomb!

———•◦•———

God's Spirit joins himself to our spirits to declare that we
are God's children.

(Romans 8.16, GNB)

What's your flammability score? You're probably just like me:
I work, as full-time as I can, as a writer. I am my husband's full-
time carer. And I also look after the house. And the garden.
And the finances. And the car. And the cooking. And the
laundry. And deal with the daily disasters. This is all familiar
to you because you're doing it too.

To keep going, because there are always things that must get
done and there's nobody else here to do them, we may have
slipped into the habit of shutting off our feelings – of exhaustion, resentment, misery, frustration – just to be able to get on
with the tasks. Unfortunately, it doesn't work. I know of no truly
leak-proof tape for emotions! And when we hit rock bottom,
that slow puncture of emotion can threaten to explode and damage us and our hard-won peace, like a suicide bomber in its
potentially devastating impact.

That's when we need to remind ourselves that we are not alone.
God sees us. We are precious people whom God's Son died
for. We matter to him. So we must matter to ourselves and be
visible to ourselves, recognizing our danger points, our signs
of exhaustion, frustration, resentment – and have ways to deal
with them before they explode.

Danger! Unexploded bomb!

Prayer

Lord Jesus, when I feel invisible and worthless, help me to remember the huge price you paid for me. In your eyes I am precious and important. You haven't forgotten me. You haven't abandoned me. You're right here with me and your strength and love are available to me. Help me to keep my heart open to you so that I can receive your help and strength.

Self-care suggestion

Stick a cheer-up text such as 'I am a child of God' on the mirror near where you clean your teeth, comb your hair . . . Look yourself in the eye and read it, aloud if you can. Now believe it!

4

Fight the good fight

———◆◆◆———

For the Spirit that God has given us does not make us timid; instead, his Spirit fills us with power, love, and self-control.

(2 Timothy 1.7, GNB)

It's strange. Before we became carers, we probably had a lot of faith and even pride in our country's health and social services. We assumed there was a safety net there to catch the needy. Until we found ourselves in that category of needing help. And suddenly we realized, as we plummeted in freefall, that there was no net. No such thing as a system to catch us. Just a collection of organizations and departments and people – all probably caring and willing to help – but nobody actually in charge, and no system – simply a maze without a route map.

Like me, you've probably used up enormous energy and a lot of time trying to fathom out the maze and get the help your loved one needs and is entitled to. It takes a while to dawn on you, but *you* have to be the person in charge, *you* have to become the expert – on your loved one's condition, and on what he or she needs or is entitled to. Now is not the time to be a shrinking violet! There's no need to be belligerent, but you'll have to be persistent – filled with power, love and self-control. The State will help you – it's not a favour, it's your and your loved one's right – but you do have to ask (and keep asking till you get the help you need).

Prayer

Thank you, Lord, that you want us to grow into strong, capable people. Help us to be determined and courageous in getting the help our loved ones need and are entitled to. Give us patience and endurance when confronted with apparently faceless bureaucracy, and grateful hearts when doors open and the way is eased for us. Bless all those in positions to help us; and go before us to lead the way.

Self-care suggestion

Try to get out in the fresh air at least once a day, even if only for a five-minute breather! If you have a garden, there will always be something new to discover, regardless of the weather. Fresh air and sunshine will lift your spirits.

5

Fire-fighting

——◆——

The LORD watches over you . . . The LORD will keep you from all harm – he will watch over your life.

(Psalm 121.5a, 7a)

I wonder if anyone's ever tried to write a job description for the at-home carer? I'd want them to include things like juggling – too many things! – and fire-fighting – dealing with the unexpected disasters that fill our days. Today, merrily juggling everything as usual, I discovered that the front door on to the street had been left open and the cat had got out. It isn't an extremely busy road but it isn't a hundred per cent safe and the cat is a quiet bed-and-back-garden cat: she's not used to busy roads and traffic. So the cat was what I had to rush to rescue today.

It seems there's always something I haven't expected, something I didn't have my eye on. As carers, we often beat ourselves up about things like this – as if we should have eyes in the back of our heads, omniscience *and* the ability to see into the future so we can forestall the disasters or catch them in time. There, put like that, I can see how unreasonable I'm being. I'm doing my best – and I'm sure you are too – which is all we can do. So no more beating ourselves up!

Prayer

Lord, there's too much for me to keep a watch over. I'm human, weak and fallible. I can't do perfect and my failures hurt and depress me. Help me to remember that you are keeping watch over me and my loved one and that I can trust you. Once more, I hand over the situation with all its worries and all my failures into your loving hands.

Self-care suggestion

Turn your hands over and look at them. Cup them together and think how much water they might hold. Not an enormous amount. Your Heavenly Father made those hands of yours and he knows how much you can hold. When you find yourself trying to cope with more than is really possible, remember, there's a much bigger pair of hands waiting to share the load. All you have to do is hand over what's getting to you.

6

Fit for purpose

Don't you know that you yourselves are God's temple and that God's Spirit lives in you?

(1 Corinthians 3.16)

When travelling by plane, does anyone pay attention any more to those in-flight demonstrations of where the emergency exits are and where the life-jackets are kept? Flying has become so commonplace that few people really read the instruction card or even watch the flight attendant carefully pointing out exit doors and showing how to pull down the oxygen mask. Just so with our own lives. We carers are just as heedless about safety measures and escape routes for ourselves. We keep going, often without enough sleep, existing on snatched meals and far too much coffee or tea. Until we hit the wall, as marathon runners would say. Because what we're doing as carers is the equivalent of a marathon. We're in it for the long haul and we need to learn to look after ourselves and pace ourselves.

We're like the panicked mother in an aeroplane that is losing pressure rapidly. We struggle to get the oxygen mask on our child – but we haven't got ours on so we haven't got enough oxygen to do the task . . . so we both suffer. Instead, we need to fit our own mask first, then we can attend to our child. The moral is clear: if we're not fit and healthy we won't be able to look after our loved ones. We're doing no one any service by running ourselves into the ground. It isn't selfish to look after yourself – in fact, it's selfish not to!

Prayer

Lord Jesus, help us to value ourselves and our own health as important and necessary resources for this caring role. Guide us to take enough rest, to eat healthily – to remember that we matter to you physically as well as spiritually!

Self-care suggestion

Can you build in to your days at least one meal a week that you don't cook – perhaps from meals on wheels, or a local restaurant that will deliver a take-away meal?

7

Forgiveness

————◆◆◆————

> Blessed is he whose transgressions are forgiven, whose sins
> are covered. Blessed is the man whose sin the LORD does
> not count against him.
>
> (Psalm 32.1, 2a)

It's weird – I just didn't recognize what was going on. I look
back and wonder why I didn't see that he was ill. Now that I
know better, I feel so sorry – for wasted time while he was
in the earliest stages when we could have got help, for wasted
energy and unhappiness on both sides. A friend said to me
recently that knowing my loved one is ill must make forgiveness easier. And that's true. In fact, there is no need for forgiveness – because there is no blame. You don't have to forgive
illness: there is only compassion – and love.

Forgiving myself is much, much harder but just as necessary.
Not spotting the symptoms seems to be quite common. Being
bewildered about what's going on and struggling to cope add
to the problems. So, let's not make our burdens worse by being
unnecessarily harsh on ourselves. This is one burden, as the
forgiven child of your loving Heavenly Father, that you don't
have to carry!

Prayer

Dear Lord, I wonder if you look at us, your sinful children, with
the same kind of compassion, understanding and love that
I now feel – at my best times – for my sick partner? Please

forgive the hurt I have caused us both through my lack of understanding, tolerance and love, and give me generously of your supplies so I can pour them out, as you pour them out on me.

Self-care suggestion

What little things always make you feel special and cherished? Make a list, choose one thing and do it! (Keep the list where you can refer to it when you feel particularly low – and don't just promise yourself that you will get round to doing something. Pick one and do it!)

8

Happy families

————◆——————

A wise son brings joy to his father, but a foolish son grief
to his mother.

(Proverbs 10.1)

Maybe you're fortunate in your family and they've been a
great help and support. For many of us it's a tough learning
curve on both sides. It's easy to forget that they too have to
go through the same difficult stages to acceptance – denial,
anger, disappointed expectations, the grief of that too-early
long bereavement – and deal with the inevitable changes in
the family relationships and the whole balance of the family.
They may have to tolerate a degree of benign neglect while
you focus on being a carer. There may be resentment . . .

This is normal. It goes with the territory. How we handle it
makes the greatest difference. And we can't handle it on our
own. Our energy may be used up with the caring task and it
seems unfair that we have to dredge up even more forgiveness,
tolerance, compassion and patience. But we are only asked to
give what we ourselves receive from our Heavenly Father, so let's
draw on his resources – and those of our church family. Have
you told them what help you need so they have the chance to
help too?

Prayer

Dear Lord, thank you for my family. Thank you for their support and love and help. When I feel they're not doing enough

or not being understanding, help me to forgive them. People live busy lives and have their own worries and concerns. Help me to be understanding. Thank you for my church family who help to fill the gaps.

Self-care suggestion

There are two things you can do that will make a difference to this situation. First, pray a blessing on the family members who are the least supportive. Second, take a step in creating your own support network by making a list of people who you can call on for practical help.

9

Here to help!

For I was hungry and you gave me something to eat, I was thirsty and you gave me something to drink, I was a stranger and you invited me in, I needed clothes and you clothed me, I was sick and you looked after me . . . whatever you did for one of the least of these brothers of mine, you did for me.

(Matthew 25.35, 40)

There are so many lovely people out there, kind and willing to help. And then there are the ones who say, 'Do call us' and, 'We're here to help!' as they turn cheerfully away leaving you no better off than before. You know these were only empty words, uttered to make the speakers feel they are nice people. And they'll be feeling better now – because they offered, didn't they?

Many a time you'll want to show what you're feeling but it's not wise. These people are impregnable in their 'nice people' armour and ear plugs. You'll only make yourself feel worse. Try instead having a little list of simple tasks that you could do with somebody else doing and offer them an easy one, well within their capabilities. That's right. Give them the opportunity to transform their words-only help into hands-on help. You may be surprised and they'll actually agree to do something. But even if they don't, you haven't lost anything. They have. And if you're feeling particularly noble, you can make yourself feel even better by praying for them.

Prayer

Dear Lord, help me to keep my cool with those people who mouth empty words but never actually do anything to help. Please forgive them. And let me be the kind of person who is a real helper to others whenever I can be.

Self-care suggestion

Tell someone who does help you how much you appreciate this help. Saying 'thank you' makes everyone feel good!

10

Heroes

Be strong and courageous. Do not be terrified; do not
be discouraged, for the LORD your God will be with you
wherever you go.

(Joshua 1.9)

Remember Superman? And the actor who played Superman,
the late Christopher Reeve? After he was paralysed, he is
reported as saying: 'When the first Superman movie came out,
I was frequently asked, "What is a hero?" My answer was that
a hero is someone who commits a courageous action without
considering the consequences – a soldier who crawls out of a
foxhole to drag an injured buddy to safety. I also meant
people who are slightly larger than life: Houdini and Lindbergh,
John Wayne, JFK and Joe DiMaggio. Now my answer is completely different. I think of a hero as an ordinary individual who
finds the strength to persevere and endure in spite of overwhelming obstacles.'

As carers, we need that strength to persevere and endure. We
need to be heroes dealing with overwhelming obstacles. But not
in our own strength. That's the way to burnout. The good
news is that we don't need to rely on ourselves. Our Heavenly
Father longs for us to rely on him for everything we need, whether it's strength, compassion, courage, patience . . .

Prayer

Dear Lord, I'm not strong and I'm not courageous. I'm more aware of my own weakness now than ever before and I am too frightened even to look ahead into the future. But I know you're there, just as I know you're here with me today. So I ask you for the strength I need for today, the courage I need to get through today. Help me to take one day at a time, confident that I can come to you and trust you to supply my needs.

Self-care suggestion

You deserve a medal. Maybe you have a brooch or a lapel pin you can designate your medal and wear it to give yourself a smile! Don't tell anyone. It's a bit of fun for you!

11

Hi ho, hi ho!

If anyone would come after me, he must deny himself and take up his cross and follow me.

(Matthew 16.24)

Many of us tried, in the early days, to explain away the symptoms in our loved ones. We grasped the flimsy straws of the good days and then crashed and burned when our hopes were dashed by another clear sign of the illness or disability.

This is not the way forward. We need acceptance. Surrender. But that is neither defeat nor defeatism. We don't need to fight what has happened but instead enfold it – and our loved ones – in love and care. This will cushion our loved ones – and ourselves – and enable us to live as happily and successfully as possible with the illness or disability. Because it won't go away. And it will probably get worse.

Resistance is a waste of energy. This is where you are today. It's your choice whether you pick up your cross and 'Hi ho, hi ho' your way into the day with a jaunty (even if forced) whistle, or bang your head against the brick wall that is the carer's life.

Prayer

Lord Jesus, I hate this disease/disability and what it's doing to us. I'm angry and want to deny that it's happening. I want to fight – or run away. But I can't do either. You ask me to take up my cross every day – to accept this situation, this burden –

but you also promise that it won't get heavier than I can carry because you're here sharing the load with me. On those terms I accept. Give me a peaceful heart and joyful acceptance, and a 'Hi ho, hi ho' to get me started on today.

Self-care suggestion

Sing or whistle – but choose a happy tune. Try some praise songs or hymns. If you're really feeling down, go for Psalm 23 – but sing it out loud. The extra oxygen will in itself give you a lift!

12

I give up

But a Samaritan . . . took pity on him. He went to him and bandaged his wounds . . . Then he put the man on his own donkey, brought him to an inn and took care of him. The next day he took out two silver coins and gave them to the innkeeper. 'Look after him,' he said, 'and when I return, I will reimburse you for any extra expense you may have.'

(Luke 10.33b–35)

For most of us, there comes a time when we cannot look after our loved ones appropriately or safely on our own at home. For some of us, our own health breaks down, and help is crucial. Bringing in a paid carer or having our loved ones go into residential care can be very painful. It feels like disloyalty. Admitting defeat. Failure. There's guilt and lots of other negative feelings. But if you've got to the stage where simply saying to yourself or a friend, 'I just can't do this any longer' gives you a feeling of relief, then it is time for a change in the way your loved one is cared for.

Struggling on when you're way past the end of your strength is no way to provide good care. It's a hard choice but for the best if your loved one will receive better quality care from someone else. You're not giving up – you're delegating. Like the good Samaritan, you continue to love and care, but in a different way. Notice how he didn't stay on for as long as the injured man needed him – he did the initial bit, then paid for

I give up

continued help, which he planned and supervised. This now becomes your role, and it is just as important, just as caring.

Prayer

Dear Lord, help me to know when it is right to bring in other carers or make the move to residential care. Guide us to the best people, the best place for my loved one. Go ahead of us and smooth the way to make the transition as easy as possible. And comfort me, Lord, as I let go.

Self-care suggestion

You may find yourself moping and not knowing what to do with your new free time. Be gentle with yourself: you're doing a kind of grieving as you let go and deal with the change in your relationship. Then use some of the new time to get real rest. Don't tackle long-ignored chores! Rest, nap and sleep are priorities. Treat yourself rather like a convalescent till you start to feel more yourself again. It takes time but it will happen.

13

It hurts

——◦——

I am in pain and despair; lift me up, O God, and save me!
... The LORD listens to those in need and does not forget his people in prison.

(Psalm 69.29, 33, GNB)

Nobody warns you that disability or degenerative illness –
whichever it is you're dealing with – *hurts*. Your loved one
who is actually enduring the condition may feel no direct pain –
but you do. What you feel will change from day to day and
moment to moment but there is a pain that lingers. It's like a
toothache, flaring up from a constant nagging ache into hot,
sharp, unbearable agony.

We each have our special mixture of exhaustion-fuelled
pain and despair, grief and disappointment, and much more.
You know your own variety. But how to deal with this pain?
Fighting it seems to make it worse. Instead, it needs to be
acknowledged, as in the psalm above. Recognized for what it
is. And – that word again – accepted. Trust that God is aware
of your pain and cares. Then simply enfold your life around
it – and, like the grit in the oyster shell, it may be transformed
into the heart of a beautiful pearl.

Prayer

Lord, give me more love to spread like balm over the hurt I
feel. Give me grace to accept my life as it is now. Give me strength

for today and joy for today that I may live even with this pain till you release me.

Self-care suggestion

Choose a treat for yourself today – one that you can enjoy, knowing that afterwards it won't leave a bitter taste (no hangover or weight gain, for example!).

14

Just a carer

The LORD your God is with you, he is mighty to save. He will take great delight in you, he will quiet you with his love, he will rejoice over you with singing.

(Zephaniah 3.17)

'And what do you do?' people ask, pretty much as the first question after you've been introduced. Do you say, 'Nothing really'? Or do you find yourself stammering as you search for something to say along the lines of, 'I look after my husband/wife/child' while watching the interest disappear in the other person's face? It's strange how undervalued being a carer is in a society that would collapse financially and practically if we stopped doing it! (Pause for a moment and allow yourself the naughty pleasure of imagining every carer in the country bringing the one they care for and parking them at the door of No. 10 Downing Street just for ten minutes! Central London would grind to a halt . . .)

People who haven't been in your situation have no idea what your task involves. Those who do it for a salary get training and qualifications. Nowadays it's possible to do a Master's degree in caring! Those of us who have had to learn on the job have no diploma to show for the hours spent finding out the hard way how to do things. But we know it's a real job requiring real and specialist skills, a tiring job that drains us physically and emotionally.

It's too easy, hidden away at home, to feel invisible and unappreciated. But your Heavenly Father sees your hard work and values you and what you are doing. Would you say you were 'just' a Christian? So you're not 'just a carer' either!

Prayer

Dear Lord Jesus, thank you for your example of service. You found no task too great or too lowly and in all that you did, from washing feet to dying on the cross, you showed the enormous value of self-giving love. Help me to follow in your footsteps and give freely of my love, knowing that you honour me and uphold me in this task of caring.

Self-care suggestion

Some organizations produce cards that state, 'I am a family carer', which will alert the necessary authority if you get run down by a bus, but are also useful for reminding yourself and others that you have a serious job and your time is valuable. Place a card somewhere visible in your purse or wallet.

15

Keeping your head above water

The apostles gathered round Jesus and reported to him all they had done and taught. Then, because so many people were coming and going that they did not even have a chance to eat, he said to them, 'Come with me by yourselves to a quiet place and get some rest.'

(Mark 6.30–31)

Do you have days when you're coping – just? Days when you could use another couple of hours' (or days') sleep, an extra pair of hands (or a few clones of yourself!) to get everything done? Those are the days when it's time to admit you're not Superman or Superwoman.

It doesn't really matter that the house is a bit of a mess. There's a roof over our heads. At the moment, it's raining heavily and the water is seeping into the garage (I must get those gutters cleared!) but I've put newspapers down to soak it up. Isn't that pretty much what we do with our lives as carers? Trying to cope with *what is*. Not fighting it. Accepting it with as peaceful a heart as we can, and then doing what we can to minimize the problems of the day, maybe even create a little joy. And one way to do that is to stop trying to be Superman or Superwoman and just be ourselves, taking a little more time to do things, cutting ourselves some slack.

Prayer

Lord Jesus, you got tired and knew the dangers of running on empty. Wisely, you took time to rest, to be with your Father and recharge, and you taught your disciples to do the same. Help me to remember that I need to do this too. You don't ask me to be Superwoman. By cutting myself some slack and taking time out to rest and be with you, I will find the strength to go on, and maybe find some joy to share.

Self-care suggestion

Just stop. For a moment. Count to five and slow your breathing. There – a micro-rest! Can you fit in another one later? Just doing nothing for one tiny moment is a small thing but a big contribution towards good self-care.

16

Let it be

---◆---

Because he himself suffered when he was tempted, he is able to help those who are being tempted.

(Hebrews 2.18)

Being a carer is tough but I've been wondering recently whether things really are as tough as I've been thinking. I'd been feeling overwhelmed but suddenly thought: is this true? Or am I creating a maelstrom of worry about the future, about potential disaster, that may never happen? Am I *thinking* myself into feeling overwhelmed?

Of course, dealing with disability or degenerative illness is overwhelming but we don't have to *be* overwhelmed. If we're finding it that hard, maybe we've fallen into the trap of making it even harder than it needs to be. We have to remember that we're not alone in this – and the trustworthy One who is with us has promised to help us so that we are not defeated. It's time to stop struggling. We don't have to exhaust ourselves to prove we're good carers. We can let that go, and instead decide to walk this journey with Jesus, who provides peace and strength and comfort.

Prayer

Lord Jesus, I open my hands and let go into your hands: my loved one, my worries, my exhaustion, my fears, my plans . . . everything. I know I can trust you to look after it all for me.

Self-care suggestion

Have you been trying to manage everything so well, organiz-ing everything down to the last item, so you feel in control? Show God you trust him to be in charge by relaxing a little on your plans. Just sit for a while instead of rushing off to the next thing on your to-do list. Demonstrate to God that you know he's in charge.

17

Let it out!

———•◆•———

I love the LORD, for he heard my voice; he heard my cry
for mercy. Because he turned his ear to me, I will call on
him as long as I live.

(Psalm 116.1–2)

Some days, some weeks even, I can cope. There are even nice
days, happy days, good days. But then there come days when
things don't go right and everything seems to build up until
I'm ready to scream, 'Stop! Let me out!'

You too?

That's okay. That's normal. And it's better to let it out than
hold it inside. But how to find somewhere safe to let it out, someone safe to say it to, without anyone being hurt – not me or
the person I'm caring for. Not everywhere is safe. Not everyone will respond with understanding and kindness. Talking to
the wrong person can do more damage. So choose wisely.

Yes, it's one more burden – discretion – to add to the constant watchfulness and other chores. But safe havens are worth
finding, and using!

Prayer

Lord, I know you love me just as much when I'm coping as
when I'm not. You want to help me. You reach out to me but
sometimes I'm so burdened I can't reach out to you. Help
me to see I don't need to carry all this alone. Let me empty
out the burdens in my arms at the foot of your cross. There

they go – all the tiredness, the over-responsibility, the constant watchfulness. There, Lord, all of it – and now I have empty arms to reach out to you and accept your loving embrace.

Self-care suggestion

When you need to let it out, try: pummelling your pillow (make sure you're alone, and if you want to yell a bit, choose a soundproof room or time when there's no one else in the house); go for a fast walk until you're ready to slow down; play loud music.

18

Living with the chaos

Ignoring what they said, Jesus told the synagogue ruler, 'Don't be afraid; just believe.'

(Mark 5.36)

There's a hymn that seems to be most people's favourite, 'Dear Lord and Father of mankind', and it used to be one of mine. Until I became a carer, when one of the lines jarred with sudden force: 'Let our ordered lives confess the beauty of your peace.' I like order. I like neatness and tidiness. I even arrange my herbs and spices in alphabetical order. But now, ordered lives? Not where I am. Being a carer teaches you that there are things more important than tidiness, than being on time, than order. Chaos is part of our life. Spills and messes are inevitable. Time becomes irrelevant: things take as long as they'll take. If a disaster happens you have to stop everything and deal with it.

Oh, we probably fight it at the start, trying to maintain the standards we had. But soon we realize that there is a full-frontal clash: we can either try to keep things the way they were, and have exhausted, unhappy lives, or accept the chaos as part of the landscape we're currently living in, and achieve a measure of peace. I reckon Jesus didn't have a Filofax or a watch. He made time for people – the haemorrhaging woman who touched his robe while Jairus was trying to hurry him to save his daughter's life. It all turned out right in the end but Jairus must have been like a cat on hot bricks! Like me when I'm clock-watching and things just don't go right. As if that matters. Jesus shows me where my focus must be.

Prayer

Thank you, Lord, for your example, showing us that people matter most and that you'll always provide exactly as much time as we need to get done the things you want us to get done. And nothing else matters! Thank you, Lord, that you're right here with us, in the middle of the chaos of our daily lives – that so long as it's a loving chaos, we're doing okay.

Self-care suggestion

If you find the chaos really painful, you can exercise your need for tidiness and control in your own space. Grant yourself a cupboard or drawer tidy-out. Having one place under control makes a big difference!

19

Me and St Stephen

———•◦•———

Jesus straightened up and asked her, 'Woman, where are they? Has no-one condemned you?'

'No-one, sir,' she said.

'Then neither do I condemn you,' Jesus declared.

(John 8.10–11)

It was one of those days. Exhaustion had set in early but there was still too much to do and only me to do it. Get help? Well, yes, of course that would be nice. In fact, someone had offered . . . But would they really be able to cope? Splash: straight into the 'easier-to-do-it-myself-even-though-I'm-totally-worn-out' trap.

We all do it. We all feel we should be able to manage, keep on keeping on regardless. And after we've pushed ourselves too far, we crumple into the inadequacy zone. After all, everyone else at carers' group seems to manage. But pushing ourselves too hard leads to exhaustion, which leads to feeling inadequate, which leads to despair and, if we're not careful, to a major attack of feeling martyred, with our apparently neglectful family and friends holding the coats.

Stop. Nobody's throwing stones – except you, yourself. You've been doing your best and probably more than that, and now you're just worn out. Nobody's going to hand out gold stars for dying on the job. In fact, if you're in danger of that, it's definitely time to stop trying to do it all yourself. Even God took a day off after creating the world.

Prayer

Remind me I'm not alone, my Lord. Remind me that you have me firmly and safely in your hands and that I can rest in you and lay down my burdens. I come to you to replenish my strength and energy. Restore my patience and my compassion, refill my heart with love.

Self-care suggestion

Have something to look forward to – a bubble bath, a new magazine, a cup of special tea – and take the time to savour it. Try for something small each day that reminds you that life is good and you are special.

20

Only the lonely

———•◆•———

Do not <u>forsake</u> your friend . . . when disaster strikes you
– better a neighbour nearby than a brother far away.
(Proverbs 27.10)

When your loved one can't get out, or only with a lot of
difficulty, your days will likely be spent mainly within the four
walls of your home (unless you're fortunate enough to have
someone to help, who can let you get out from time to time).
Even though the person you're caring for is there, let's admit
that doesn't really seem like company. After all, you can hardly
share exactly how you're feeling with your loved one. As a result,
you become lonely and isolated – all carers do, unless they make
a lot of effort to go out.

But once you're out, people ask you how things are – and
the big temptation is to tell them! Sadly, even with the best will
in the world, friends can find the recitation of your woes
tedious. Family can feel threatened or guilty. The result is an
even greater feeling of being all alone in the world with this
terrible burden. You can plummet down into feeling that
you're the only person in the universe suffering like this.

Not true. It's just that you've slipped to the bottom of the
pit of despair and loneliness and can't see over the top. Getting
isolated and feeling desperately lonely go with the territory –
but it's dangerous for your physical and mental health. Remember, isolation is used as punishment and torture! God declared
it wasn't good for people to be isolated so he thoughtfully

matched up Adam and Eve as company for each other. I know it's difficult to make yourself go out when you've got into the habit of being shut in, and it's hard reaching out to people when you're lonely, but it's essential. Remember, you're worth it!

Prayer

Lord Jesus, even though you enjoyed time spent alone with your Father, you needed friends too and chose twelve to accompany you. Please encourage my friends to rally round and give me the company and the outlet for my feelings that I need. Help me not to monopolize our meetings with my worries and moans. Let me be a good friend to them too!

Self-care suggestion

If you can get out, choose a place where there are lots of people – a shopping mall, a park. Just sit for a few minutes and smile at anyone who smiles at you!

21

Ouch! I'm trying to help . . .

———•◦•———

If it is possible, as far as it depends on you, live at peace with everyone.

(Romans 12.18)

I saw a woman in the supermarket yesterday. She had the generally washed-out look of the overexhausted long-term carer and was hurrying to get her shopping done. Then I noticed the tell-tale too-pale make-up on her cheek where she was trying to hide a bruise. Sometimes the ones we're caring for don't have full control over their limbs and an arm or leg too easily makes sudden contact. While unpleasant, this is readily forgivable (on our better days!). But sometimes, sadly, a stage is reached in the illness where outbursts, accusations of stealing and evil intent, and actual violence make life even harder to bear.

It's not easy to remember, when faced with verbal or physical abuse, that it is usually even more horrible for our loved ones who are lashing out in wordless fear and anger at their own illness and disability. We just happen to be the closest.

Turning the other cheek, trying to maintain peace and harmony, is difficult but trying to respond to the underlying feelings rather than to the bizarre or unpleasant behaviour will help you to get through.

Prayer

Dearest Lord, I need your strength and patience, your long-suffering love, to get me through this stage. I'm finding it hard but just knowing that you're here with me in it, holding me up, knowing I'm doing my best, does help me. Please help me to be kind and compassionate rather than quick with indignation!

Self-care suggestion

How you defuse your feelings will depend on how unjust and nasty the offending behaviour was. I have a friend who got through three swingballs! Just writing it down may be enough. Seeing it in black and white puts things in perspective. Most of all, you may need some time out – even if only five minutes in another room – to stop you saying anything you'd regret later!

22

Rags, and losing them

In your anger, do not sin.

(Ephesians 4.26a)

I like to think of myself as basically an okay person – and I'm sure that you are much better than okay! But one of the things I dislike most about being a carer is that it shows me up to myself in the worst possible light – I seem to do so much wrong! And today I'm feeling angry. I think first of all I'm angry with God about this illness and the effect it's having on us and our lives. Then I'm angry with the doctors who brushed us aside. If only we'd had a diagnosis earlier . . . And of course I'm angry with myself because I didn't realize there was something really wrong until it was staring me in the face.

But the worst thing about my anger is that I do get cross and impatient with my loved one. Sometimes it seems as if he's doing things purposely (yes, I know he's not!) and then I get very angry with myself for losing my rag with him. It's a vicious circle and once on it, it seems very difficult to get off and create peace again. But I do recognize that's in my current job description. It's up to me to create the atmosphere in our home and regardless of how I feel, we need to be living in peace and calmness. So it's time to bite the bullet and go and apologize again, smooth ruffled feathers and pour oil.

Prayer

Lord Jesus, you know my weaknesses. I am so sorry that I lost my patience and my control, and let fly with harsh words. Please forgive me. Cleanse me from my sin and give me strength to stay calm. You promised us peace and I ask for that peace now – peace in my heart and peace in my home and peace in my dealings with my loved one.

Self-care suggestion

When you're on the verge of saying something you'll regret, when the anger or resentment is bubbling up inside like a volcano ready to blow its top, divert that energy. A friend used to keep empty jam jars by the back door of her house and she would rush to the bottom of her garden and smash them inside a safe container. Bottle banks are great for this! Scrubbing something clean is a good defuser. You may find that cutting down on the caffeine helps you to stay calmer. And pray!

23

Running on empty

Those who hope in the Lord will renew their strength. They will soar on wings like eagles; they will run and not grow weary, they will walk and not be faint.

(Isaiah 40.31)

One of the biggest problems and danger areas for carers is tiredness. Exhaustion. Bone-deep weariness that makes you want to sit and weep. This is when you know you're running on empty.

It's strange. We don't shout at our car when it needs to be filled up with petrol, but we do tend to be harsh with ourselves when we're worn out and there's still too much to do. Stop. Think petrol. That's all it is. You're running on empty and that's not really possible. When you run your car down to the last dregs, you're in danger of getting nasty grungy bits stuck in your engine where they can do damage. Same with us. Toxic stuff begins to appear. Obviously, the best thing is never to let the tank get empty – but as any carer knows, that's simply not realistic.

We all get overexhausted. It goes with the territory. Learn to recognize your weak points and be as accepting of them as you are of the needle on your car that says when your tank is running low. And then do what you do with your car: take it to where you'll get it filled again!

Prayer

Lord, I'm asking, trusting that you hear me and that you do care about me. What I need today is . . . (*Write your own list.*

Write it down and date it. When you look back, in a week or a month or even at the end of the day, you'll be awed by God's love and provision for you, answering your needs in ways more wonderful than you could have imagined.) Thank you, faithful Lord, who hears my prayers.

Self-care suggestion

Who else can you ask to do something to help you? Reaching out to others is not weakness but strength. Make a list of what you need help with and then alongside each item jot down the name of anyone you think might realistically be able and willing to help out, even a little. Then choose one – the one you feel most hopeful about – and ask!

24

Sharing the load

———•◆•———

Come to me, all you who are weary and burdened, and I
will give you rest. Take my yoke upon you and learn from
me, for I am gentle and humble in heart, and you will find
rest for your souls. For my yoke is easy and my burden is
light.

(Matthew 11.28–29)

We get so used to going it alone that it can be very difficult to
switch off when we finally get some help and some time to ourselves. I've got a respite break at the moment (to let me write
this book!) and I feel restless, edgy, guilty – not very helpful
emotions. Here, alone in the quiet, I am suddenly aware of how
I'm on the alert all the time, listening out for problems, the
adrenaline coursing through my system.

Maybe I've been carrying too much for too long and have
not really been leaning on God the way he invites us to. Our
yoke-partner doesn't ask *us* to do all the work – just our share –
and to trust him to do his, which will always be the lion's
share!

I wonder, is it because we underestimate God's willingness
to help us that we don't ask? Do we trust that he loves us and
wants to help? Or do we underestimate his ability to help? Surely
we can learn to trust the Creator of the universe, Source of all
that is? He gave his beloved Son for us. What I need now is
small compared to that!

Prayer

Lord, maybe I make the way harder for myself than it need be. Help me to practise dropping my burdens at your feet each morning as I wake and throughout the day. Remind me you are my yoke-mate and you have broad shoulders and strong arms that are well able to carry the load for me. Thank you, Lord.

Self-care suggestion

I have a friend who taught her children to distinguish which things they should attend to and which were SEPs: Somebody Else's Problem. This was to teach them personal responsibility and wisdom about unwarranted interference. In our role as carers, we need to recognize what is ours to carry and what is God's. Maybe a code like SEP would help. What about TOG: This One's God's – perhaps that would remind us not to try and carry everything!

25

Snakes and ladders

———◆———

Those who sow in tears will reap with songs of joy. He who goes out weeping, carrying seed to sow, will return with songs of joy, carrying sheaves with him.

(Psalm 126.5–6)

Elisabeth Kübler-Ross, the pioneer in helping people face death and bereavement, reckoned that five stages are involved: denial, anger, bargaining, depression and acceptance. And she felt it was important to experience each stage fully to enable us to move on towards acceptance, otherwise we can get stuck in depression. This pattern is so familiar to carers. We cycle round and round the five stages. Just when we think we've achieved some measure of acceptance, we find we've slid back down the snake of anger, and the ladder back up to acceptance seems far too high and far away!

Where are you today on the snakes and ladders of being a carer? Blocked emotions block progress, block healing, block wholeness. Unblocking releases energy – what you're not using to fight off those feelings will be available for everything else you've got to do!

Prayer

Lord Jesus, sliding down snakes is so much easier – and familiar to me – than climbing up ladders! Thank you that you don't expect me to be a mountain climber. You know who I am and what I'm capable of and you meet me right where I am even if to me it feels like being back at Square One! Thank you that you are the Lord of new beginnings. Square One is a good place to be with you!

Self-care suggestion

Do something silly. Have a go at the swings in your local playground, roll up your trouser legs and go for a paddle, buy yourself a drippy ice cream cone. Whatever. Choose something silly and childlike and fun and give yourself a smile today.

26

Someone to lean on

———◆———

Trust in the LORD with all your heart [and mind] and lean
not on your own understanding.

(Proverbs 3.5)

Trust in the LORD for ever, for the LORD, the LORD, is
the Rock eternal.

(Isaiah 26.4)

Watching television the other day, I was reminded about the
fashion for outdoor artificial ice rinks. I love to watch how someone goes on the ice for the first time, very wobbly, but then
a friend comes alongside, takes the learner's arm and together
they step out. Gradually the new skater learns balance and confidence and soon they're gliding along.

It came to me that life for a carer is a bit like an ice rink. We
step out, unsure and very wobbly. We fall over and have lots of
bumps. But God asks us to lean on him – and then it gets a
little easier. I won't say we glide off in carefree beauty but it
does get better! We'll get there and though life is slippery, we
have a Friend to lean on. He's just waiting.

Prayer

Dearest Lord, I am so glad that you are my partner in this
hazardous journey of care. So often I try to go it alone and
fall flat on my face. Please forgive me. I welcome the hand you
offer to help me get up on my feet again and I love the idea of

slipping my arm into yours and letting you guide me forwards. Thank you for the hope and renewed confidence that gives me.

Self-care suggestion

If this idea of the ice rink helps you, there's a lovely painting by Scottish artist Sir Henry Raeburn showing the Victorian Reverend Robert Walker skating on Duddingston Loch, hands tucked into a muff. You could get a postcard of it to pin up to remind yourself of your heavenly partner in this slippery phase of your life! If this picture doesn't appeal, you could look out for one that does – something inspirational or simply cheerful!

27

Stormy weather

He replied, 'You of little faith, why are you so afraid?' Then he got up and rebuked the winds and the waves, and it was completely calm.

(Matthew 8.26)

It is easy to get lost in the midst of the overwhelming, all-consuming task of caring for someone. The 36-hour day saps all our energy and we hardly recognize that exhausted face we catch a glimpse of in the mirror. Did you have time to comb your hair this morning before the first upset that needed your hundred per cent concentration? And was that really you patiently, quietly dealing with it? Later in the day, was that you too who then lost it completely over another upset?

In any one day, we can experience the full range of emotional highs and lows. It can be like struggling to cope in a small boat without oars on a stormy sea! One of my favourite hymns has a chorus that begins, 'We have an anchor'. I think we all need that anchor safely and securely fastened to Jesus, who is that Rock who will not move during the stormy weather of this stage in our lives and the illness or disability of our loved ones. All we have to do is reach out – he waits, patiently, for our call.

Prayer

Dearest Lord, I have accepted this task of caring for my loved one, so I cannot ask you to take all the storms away. I know they are part of this illness/disability. Instead, please keep me firmly anchored to you so I can go on coping and caring.

Self-care suggestion

Have you managed to comb your hair/clean your teeth/do anything at all for yourself today? Stop! Do it at once. You'll feel much better if you ensure a few moments to get clean and tidy and presentable.

28

Surely this can't be right?

—◆—

'I know the plans I have for you,' declares the LORD, 'plans to prosper you and not to harm you, plans to give you hope and a future.'

(Jeremiah 29.11)

Some days I wake up calm, even cheerful about my life. More often I'm floundering in the morass and the thought pops up, 'Surely this can't be right? Surely God can't want this for me?' This is a nasty trick of the opposition to get us to wallow in a pit of treacly misery and descend into hopelessness and depression. In no time I'm focused solidly on myself, how bad it is for me and so on . . . and I've subtracted God from the equation – because surely this can't be his will for me? He couldn't be that cruel.

Where I need to be is back on solid ground, trusting that God truly is in charge of my life and that everything will work out. And the only bridge between the miserable pit my negative thinking dumps me in and that safe solid ground of reassurance is Jesus. It's an extreme example but I remember the thief on the cross next to Jesus, who must have been reviewing one very misspent life – and Jesus was able to reassure him: 'Today you will be with me in paradise.' Somehow that gets my worries into perspective, and I can pick up my cross and continue in the knowledge that I *am* where God wants me to be.

Prayer

Dear Lord, please forgive my doubts and fretting. Don't let me get overwhelmed. Help me instead to cling to you, the Rock of my salvation, and help me build my life on that solid ground.

Self-care suggestion

If you worry that you're suffering because you've got things wrong, take five minutes to confess this to God. Confess everything and ask for forgiveness – and be assured that you will be forgiven. Then choose something that means *new* to remind you that all is forgiven and you step out anew in God's love and purpose for you.

29

Telling it how it is

He who listens to you listens to me; he who rejects you
rejects me; but he who rejects me rejects him who sent
me.

(Luke 10.16)

Most people, when they stop to ask how things are, usually
ask how your loved one is. They seldom ask how *you* are. But
when they do, what do you say? If you're like most of us, you
mutter, 'I'm okay.' You've learned that they don't really want to
know that you're chewing the mantelpiece with frustration
at what your loved one has taken to doing most recently, or
that you're falling asleep every time you sit down (and that
includes in the loo). They smile cheerfully and say something
like, 'Good for you', and off they go.

And you're ready to take a bite out of whatever's nearest –
because it's your own fault. They believed you. So they won't
offer to help. Or sympathize. Or anything. You're on your own.
Head-banging doesn't help. You've probably already got a head-
ache. Telling it like it is will. But choose your listeners carefully. There are people who do care enough to be told the whole
story and there are people whose eyes will glaze over as they
frantically search for a way to get away, leaving you feeling like
the Ancient Mariner.

You don't have to go for the jugular with the goriest details.
Something brief and simple that opens the window on life as
it really is for you can be a stepping stone to firmer friendships

and real support. Telling God how it really is for you can be the start of a fresher, stronger relationship with him too. After all, he already knows so there's no point pretending. Tell it like it is!

Prayer

Thank you, Lord, that I don't have to pretend with you. I can scream and yell and howl and whinge and complain and let my feelings out in complete safety. You know what's going on. You see it all. It's such a relief to be able to be totally open when I spend my days keeping my feelings in check. Help me discern wisely who I can talk to about my life. Send me safe, loving friends who will hear me out patiently and offer support and wise counsel.

Self-care suggestion

Practise what you will say next time someone asks you how you are. Aim for cheerful, factual and non-self-pitying. And do it – at least once. See what a difference it makes to how you feel!

30

That's no way to speak to yourself!

> Therefore, there is now no condemnation for those who are in Christ Jesus, because through Christ Jesus the law of the Spirit of life set me free from the law of sin and death.
>
> (Romans 8.1)

Guilt. It lurks, waiting for the inevitable: you get exhausted and say something less than kind, do something unfriendly. You find yourself blaming your loved one for your feeling of being trapped. You get cross with him/her for being uncooperative or just plain nasty.

You feel guilty that you're not doing this caring as well as the person you met at the carers' group – or as well as you'd like to. You feel guilty because you've handed over your responsibilities to a paid carer who comes in to help and seems to be doing so much better than you. You feel guilty because you just can't cope any more and you feel it's really time for your loved one to be cared for in a residential home. You feel guilty because you're actually enjoying the freedom and time off during your respite break.

There is so much we can feel guilty about – from our distaste about some of the tasks caring involves (*see* 33 'The messy stuff') to our fear of what may be round the corner. Secretly – and maybe not very deep down – we think we're selfish, failures, bad, even. What's actually happening is a nasty attack of the guilts. And it's wholly unnecessary. You're probably doing your very best, like the rest of us. But you're not perfect. So you will get things wrong. You will have bad days. Bad moments. We all do. And when we mess up, we can ask God for forgiveness. What we have to learn is to leave it there and not go digging up our failures to brood over. If he's forgiven us, the matter is over and done with, and we can get on with our jobs, doing the best we can, in his strength.

Prayer
Dear Lord, you know how often I mess up and get things wrong, how often I am unloving, impatient, thoughtless . . . I ask for your forgiveness (*mention anything in particular that's on your conscience*). Help me not to judge myself but leave that to you, who are kind and ever patient with us, ever forgiving. Thank you that you forgive my sins. Thank you that I can go on, forgiven and cleansed and strengthened.

Self-care suggestion
Some of us have more sensitive consciences than others. You know who you are! If something is particularly bugging you, write it on a piece of paper, ask God's forgiveness and then burn it (safely!) to underline that it's now forgiven and gone. It helps to keep short accounts with God – asking forgiveness the minute you've done or said something that you regret, or before you go to sleep each night.

31

The evolving carer

————◆·◆·◆————

The LORD will guide you always; he will satisfy your
needs in a sun-scorched land and will strengthen your
frame. You will be like a well-watered garden, like a
spring whose waters never fail.

(Isaiah 58.11)

Some professionals refer to the experience of caring as a journey – and it is; it is a journey with your loved one as their illness or disability progresses, and they need more or less care.
But it is a journey in which we make progress too.

At first, we have to deal with the diagnosis and the impact
it will make on our lives. I hated it when those carers farther
on down the line told me confidently, 'You'll cope.' I was so afraid
that I wouldn't. I knew I couldn't cope with what they were dealing with. But now I realize I have coped – coped with much
more than I could ever have imagined.

We adapt. I flailed at first – raged against the illness, how it
disrupted my life. I flailed about, trying to care, not knowing
how to do this thing called caring. I read every book I could
lay my hands on – and despaired. And I prayed. Not always po-
lite, please-and-thank-you prayers but angry, passionate, it's-not-
fair prayers and I-just-can't-cope prayers. And, somehow, I
found myself coping. I found people turning up to help me. I
discovered that God had been farther down the road setting up
what we needed. All I had to do was trust, and keep going to
the best of my ability. And that's all he asks of you.

Prayer

Thank you, Lord, that you have walked this road with me every step of the way. You've gone ahead of us and prepared the path, so often so amazingly! You've supported us and helped us and got us through this far – and I know you'll be there all the rest of the way. Lord, I rest my hand in yours. Where you lead, I will go. I will trust in you.

Self-care suggestion

It may help you to keep a diary, a journal, where you record what's happening and how you're feeling, how you're coping. You can write your prayers here too. This is for no one's eyes but yours so it can be the whole unvarnished truth. You'll be amazed, when you read it back later, how many good days there were and how well you coped! It will also strengthen your faith as you see how God has been working in your life.

32

The key to getting help

You do not have what you want because you do not ask God for it.

(James 4.2b, GNB)

When I was young, clamouring for something that took my fancy, my grandmother used to say: 'Wants never gets.' That effectively silenced those demands! In our situation as carers, though, I think we need to change it to, 'If you don't ask, you won't get!'

I had an example this morning – an email from someone thanking me for letting him know my husband had moved into a care home for a few weeks. 'Say hello to him for me,' he finished. I was outraged. Surely the least he could do was go and visit him and say hello for himself! I confess I rewrote my reply several times, toning it down until it was fit to send. In the end I simply asked him to visit if he could manage it, leaving the request open and without barbs.

We have to bury both our shrinking-violet and our self-sufficient selves. What we're asking for is not a favour for ourselves. It's needed help for our loved ones. So, don't wait for offers – you may wait for ever. You need to be specific, clear and determined. Decide exactly what it is reasonable to ask someone for, and ask! If they say no, thank them graciously and ask someone else. And don't forget about straight talking with God too – he won't be offended if the version he gets could do with toning down!

Prayer

Thank you, my Heavenly Father, that you want me to bring my shopping list of requests, my long screed of complaints and moans and miseries to you. Your ear is always there for me and you long to shower blessings on me. When I do get round to asking, you always amaze me with your providence – what you organize is always so much better than I could have dreamed. Thank you for being my Father!

Self-care suggestion

Take a little time to think about what someone else could do to help you. What haven't you got round to doing? What's niggling at you, worrying you? Keep a small notebook and every time something like that occurs to you, put it in the book. Then consider who you know who could tackle one of these tasks. Carry the notebook around with you and when you meet up with that person, ask them. The worst they can do is say no.

33

The messy stuff

————•◆•————

> So he got up from the meal, took off his outer clothing,
> and wrapped a towel round his waist. After that, he
> poured water into a basin and began to wash his disci-
> ples' feet, drying them with the towel that was wrapped
> round him.
>
> (John 13.4–5)

Unless you are very fortunate, you'll have to deal with the messy
stuff sooner or later. We're talking incontinence here. (Is this
the only 'religious' book to deal with such basics?) Paid carers
seem to manage these tasks without embarrassment or distaste
but for those of us cleaning up a parent or a spouse, it can be
very difficult. For a start, we may feel that what we are doing
is taboo or a breach of what's permitted. In the current situation it's necessary, but we may be only too aware of the indig-
nity, the embarrassment, we expect them to be feeling.

Often those feelings are ours alone and we need to deal with
them if we're going to get through this stage without further
distress to our loved ones. I am so grateful to the inventor of
yellow rubber gloves, air freshener and packaged disinfectant
wipes for floors and surfaces. A handy supply of newspapers
and bin bags helps too. Music and cheerful irrelevant chat
and an open window for gulps of fresh air will help you get
through.

And you will get through. Disgust, distaste – those may rear
their ugly heads but so will compassion and pity. You can't leave

your loved one in a mess so you roll up your sleeves. Isn't that what God did for us?

Prayer

Lord Jesus, we know you washed your disciples' mucky feet. Roads weren't smooth clean tarmac – there were donkeys, horses and camels leaving evidence of their journeys so those feet would have been pretty smelly. Yet you chose to take the lowliest place and you did this as a sign of your love and as an example to follow. Lord, I balk at some of the things I have to do but I know you can give me the strength and composure to get through. Let me remember that I am showing your love, so when all is clean again, I can offer a reassuring hug.

Self-care suggestion

When the task is done (and it is always better to finish it completely so there's no trace or smell remaining), go outside and do some breathing exercises in the fresh air: breathe in through your nose on a count of four, hold it for four, then breathe out in a big blast as if blowing out candles on a cake. Do this several times. The way to remember this instant anti-stress technique is 'smelling the roses, blowing out candles'.

34

Thorns and thistles

———◆———

Do not be afraid, though briers and thorns are all around
you and you live among scorpions.

(Ezekiel 2.6b)

Life seems to sprout thorns and thistles when you're respons-
ible for caring for someone else, especially if it wasn't originally
your role to deal with money matters and the like. If you now
have to fill in the forms on behalf of your loved one, look after
the finances, see the bills are paid, make decisions, it can feel
like you're struggling through a tangled jungle where there
are penalty-laden pitfalls for the innocent but unwary. I hit it
with getting the Enduring Power of Attorney registered. I think
we're nearly there but it took several weeks of worry, hassle and
heartache – all pretty much unnecessary if we'd only managed
better communication. It didn't help that various family members' legal advisers had different opinions and ideas.

Getting the right advice is invaluable. The tangle is so thick
you do need an experienced and well-informed guide. The
relevant charity for your loved one's disability or illness may
provide advocates and advisers. These people are worth their
weight in gold! They've seen it all before and know exactly what's
involved in the financial and legal aspects of caring. Carers'
groups are filled with 'been-there-got-the-T-shirt' experts happy
to share what they've learned. Who knows? One day you may
be the one able to share your hard-won wisdom with a new
kid on the block!

Prayer

It can feel daunting, trying to handle the legal stuff and manage the finances. I want to do what is best for my loved one but it's one more task that I don't have energy for. Lord Jesus, you told us to render to Caesar what was Caesar's. Help me to deal correctly with Caesar but to lean on you for the resources I need. Help me to identify the trustworthy advisers I need, and please go ahead and make the way smooth for me.

Self-care suggestion

If you haven't found a carers' support group yet, now might be a good time. Check your local library and doctor's surgery for notices about meetings. You may feel it's impossible to get out to a meeting but it's well worth making the effort. You'll find a welcome from people who really understand what you're going through and are happy to let you talk about it. There are friends here and a special fellowship. You may feel you don't need this – but perhaps there's someone there who needs what you have learned?

35

Time off

———◆———

Then Jesus made the disciples get into the boat and go
on ahead to the other side of the lake, while he sent the
people away. After sending the people away, he went up a
hill by himself to pray. When evening came, Jesus was there
alone.

(Matthew 14.22–23, GNB)

I'm starting the week refreshed. I'm feeling much calmer and
more able to cope because I took the whole of yesterday 'off' –
just like people who have salaried jobs and get a day off! It was
wonderful. Outside it poured with rain and I didn't mind at
all. I sat indoors and read and rested. I cooked easy, delicious
meals. And now I feel so much better.

And today maybe it's because I'm calm and relaxed that my
loved one is also calm and relaxed. He even went voluntarily
for a little nap in the afternoon.

It's easy to feel guilty about wanting time off, about needing some time for yourself. It's also easy to become overtired,
burnt out and resentful. But it's not necessary. As the passage
from Matthew shows, Jesus himself models a healthy pattern
of taking time out when it is needed.

Prayer

Thank you, Lord Jesus, for these oases that you provide along
the way. Help me to use them and benefit from them. It's too
easy a temptation to pretend to be Superman or Superwoman

and make myself keep going – but even you needed time out, and you knew your disciples needed time off, so I definitely do too! Thank you for the blessing of times of refreshment.

Self-care suggestion

Remember that when you accept God's gift of time off, you honour the giver. When you reject it, you are setting yourself up in opposition to God's knowledge of you and care for you. Does that make it easier to give yourself permission to take some time off?

36

Time out means time out!

'Martha, Martha,' the Lord answered, 'you are worried and upset about many things, but only one thing is needed. Mary has chosen what is better, and it will not be taken away from her.'

(Luke 10.41–42)

You know the feeling: you want to take some time out. You *need* to take some time out. But when you get a few moments alone and you try just to sit quietly and rest, all the things you haven't done start shouting at you. When you attempt to silence them by telling them that you'll get to them when you stand up again, and then try to quiet your mind once more, the worries, the niggles and the big concerns start buzzing round inside your head like a swarm of wasps around a saucer of jam.

Worse than that, when we get some proper respite – half a day, a day or longer – the temptation is to get stuck into all the chores that have slipped till now. It's easy to get caught out like this and before we know it our precious time has gone. So here is another discipline – this time for *our* benefit! Time out means just that. No chores. No fretting. Time out.

Prayer

As I try to settle down to some time alone with you, Lord Jesus, I need your help just to settle quietly. Help me to lay down my burdens – the mental as well as the physical ones – and simply be with you. Help me have some Mary time out of my Martha day.

Self-care suggestion

When your mind buzzes with worries and things to do, say firmly inside your head: STOP. Then breathe in deeply to the count of four. Breathe out to the count of four. Then hold that emptiness and count to four again, before taking the next breath. The physical slowing down of your breathing will calm your blood pressure. The conscious focus on your breathing will silence the inner noise. Temporarily, maybe, but every little helps!

37

Unwelcome visitors

———◆———

When you lie down, you will not be afraid; when you lie
down, your sleep will be sweet . . . for the LORD will be your
confidence.

(Proverbs 3.24, 26a)

I worry. I wake in the middle of the night in a panic. All sorts
of things rush into my barely awake brain, one after another,
till there's a flood of them and I can't get back to sleep. Then
I start to panic about not getting back to sleep. I need my sleep!
Do you have times like this?

Having total responsibility for another human being, and
one with special needs for care and support, is fraught with
worry. Or it can be. How I'd love to be like the swan, gliding
gracefully through my days (and sleeping soundly at night),
even though I may be paddling furiously below the surface!

Worry doesn't help me or my loved one. It only makes
things worse. So often, when I've handed the worries over to
my Lord, I discover everything has worked out perfectly and
I didn't need to worry about it at all! I have to accept that it's
my choice to entertain those unwelcome visitors. Instead, I have
to practise opening up and sharing them with God, and other
carers. That will defuse their power to hurt me and damage the
quality of life my loved one can enjoy.

Prayer

Dear Lord, I worry. I fret. I foresee problems where as yet there aren't any. Here, Lord – take these worries. They just burden me! I entrust my loved one into your care today. Keep him/her safe. And give me rest from worry today.

Self-care suggestion

Can you get out for a short walk? It doesn't matter if it's raining. Grab ten minutes round the garden or round the block, and play I spy: I spy with my little eye – three things to praise God for. You'll be surprised at how a switch of focus turns off the static of worry that's been besieging your mind.

38

Valley walking

———◆·◉·◆———

Even though I walk through the valley of the shadow of death, I will fear no evil, for you are with me; your rod and your staff, they comfort me.

(Psalm 23.4)

I'd been feeling really down for days. Even though he seemed not too bad. Then I realized that what I was doing was grieving. Dementia takes your loved one away from you as truly as divorce or death. The only difference is that your loved one is still there, so you can't let your feelings out and get them healed. The result: a festering wound.

The person you knew and loved has pretty well gone and in his or her place is this new, unpredictable, and sometimes scary, stranger. Many other illnesses have a similar result. And you're supposed to go on as if nothing has happened. It's as though aliens have landed in the neighbourhood and done a selective people-swap and your loved one got swapped and this alien has taken his or her place. What you're feeling is a sense of loss and you're grieving.

The experience of dementia has been called 'the long bereavement' and it is, as are many other degenerative illnesses. The only way to deal with the grief of bereavement is to face it squarely and give yourself permission to feel the feelings till they're ready to go away. Is that what you're doing? That's okay. Me too. You're not alone, and the One who said, 'Blessed are those who mourn' is at your side to support you in this as in everything else.

Prayer

Lord Jesus, you are no stranger to grief and pain and loss and I know you walk this road with me. Help me to accept the loss of what was in the past and show me that there is a future with joy. Take me by the hand and lead me there because at the moment I'm groping in the darkness. Shine your light on my path.

Self-care suggestion

Recognize what you're doing: grieving for what might have been. Then turn it round and make a list of the good memories from the past that you have to treasure. Say thank you to God for the good times. If it's appropriate, chat about it with your loved one and thank him or her. Feel the glow. Then move on into your day.

39

Whose life is it anyway?

For I am the LORD, your God, who takes hold of your right hand and says to you, Do not fear; I will help you.

(Isaiah 41.13)

Becoming a 24/7 at-home carer involves a lot of changes. Life gets to be pretty well unrecognizable, and as for us – our very identities may be changed. Once we may have been well-paid and valued employees; now we struggle to make ends meet. Once we were happily married; now we don't get enough sleep and the relationship we once knew has vanished for ever. If we're caring for a parent, the parent/child relationship and responsibilities have been turned upside down. And a mother may find herself becoming a nurse to her dependent child.

Homes need to be adapted. Once-private finances have to be opened up for those in authority to decide whether or not we qualify for benefits. Expectations have to be down-shifted. Plans have to be put on hold, or shelved permanently, as the future becomes a place we just don't want to look at. The world seems to have shifted on its axis and then settled down somewhere much less safe.

It's only now that we realize how much we value the quiet, uneventful life! Oh, for those 'green pastures and quiet waters by'! That's not where we are. We're in the scary bit. But we know that we are just as much in God's loving hand in this stage as we were when the sun shone – if not more so. When things are tough, we cling to him that much more closely and know he will never fail us.

Prayer

Thank you, my Father, that you walk with me through this difficult stage in my life. You uphold me and watch over me as I flail and struggle when there's no need. You are my refuge and my strength. I have committed myself to your love and care and that's where I want to stay!

Self-care suggestion

Collect Bible verses and fridge magnets that remind you that God loves you and he's in charge, and place them where you'll see them several times in the day. Allow yourself to read, watch or listen only to cheerful things! Banish every form of gloom – including gloomy people – from your life.

40

You need love too

The entire law is summed up in a single command: 'Love your neighbour as yourself.'

(Galatians 5.14)

Yes, of course that's what it's about. You're the carer because you do care. It is love that prompts you, motivates you, keeps you going. But sometimes it can feel like all that love has been used up and there's none left and you're on autopilot. It's sheer determination that's keeping you keeping on.

But have you noticed that the text about loving one another contains the crucial phrase 'as yourself'? That's right – you need love too. How much love are you currently receiving? If the person you're caring for is your spouse or a parent, then a major source of love may have all but dried up. In that case you need to compensate for the loss.

I'm not suggesting that you find an alternative person – for example, in an affair! It's your love for yourself that must fill the gap. How much love are you giving yourself? If the needle on your loving-yourself tank is on empty, you can't expect to have any love to give away. Time to redress the balance.

Prayer

Lord Jesus, we find it perfectly reasonable that we should be your hands and feet in this world to care for other people – but we forget we also need to be your hands and feet to look after and love ourselves. Help us to give ourselves permission to be kind to ourselves too.

Self-care suggestion

Write the numbers 1 to 20 down one side of a page and then make a list of things you love. My list might include choc ices, splashy waves, snowflakes, cats, cosy crime novels, roaring fires in the hearth on a cold night, hot chocolate, bubble baths, Stourhead, country walks. Add anything that makes you smile, or used to make you smile. And then choose one . . . and plan it into this week.

Index

Index

mess 30, 36
micro-rest 31
misery 6, 56
money matters 68
music 35

nap 25
negative thinking 56
neglect 16, 38

order 36
over-responsibility 35
overwhelmed, feeling 32
oxygen 23
oxygen masks 11
oyster shell 26

pain 26, 77
panic 74
parent, caring for 78, 80
patience 16, 20, 39, 42, 45
peace 32, 36, 42, 44, 45
pearl 26
persistence 8
perspective 43
petrol 46
pillow pummelling 35
pity 66
power 8
praise songs 23
Princess Royal Trust for
    Carers ix
providence 65
Psalms 3, 23

Raeburn, Sir Henry 53
Reeve, Christopher 20
refreshment 70
relationship, changes in 16,
    25, 78

resentment 3, 6, 16, 45, 70
resistance 22
respite break 48, 60, 72
responsibility 2, 74
rest 2, 13, 25, 31, 39

safe havens 34
safety net 8
Samaritan 24
saying 'thank you' 19
self-control 8
selfishness 12
SEPs 49
service 29
sharing the load 23
sing 23
slack, cutting some 30, 31
sleep 25, 30, 74, 78
'smelling the roses, blowing out
    candles' 67
snakes and ladders 50–1
social services 8
spills 36
spouse, caring for 80
State, the ix, 2, 8
storms 54
strength 3, 7, 20, 21, 31, 32, 39,
    42, 47, 61, 67
stress ix
sunshine 9
Superman 20, 30, 70
Superwoman 30, 31, 70
support 59; network 17
surrender 22
symptoms 22

taboo 66
take-away meal 13
tidiness 37
time 3, 30, 36; off 2, 70–1;

85